GW00702782

Talking with My Brother

John McGuckian

SUMMER PALACE PRESS

First published in 2002 by

Summer Palace Press
Cladnageeragh, Kilbeg, Kilcar, County Donegal, Ireland

© John McGuckian, 2002

Printed by Nicholson & Bass Ltd.

A catalogue record for this book is available
from the British Library

ISBN   0   95359   12   8   X

Where many a day he stood there by my side
To view the hills and fields we knew so well …
With her he loved when they were fresh and young

'For My Father'
P. J. McGuckian

Acknowledgments

Some of the poems in this book have appeared in: *Gown; Poetry Ireland Review; New Irish Writing; Ulster Tatler; Tangier; Outlines; Festschrift for William Wiser; Force 10; The Andersonstown News; HU.*

Biographical Note
John McGuckian was born in Ballymena, County Antrim and educated at St. MacNissi's College, Garron Tower, and Queen's University, Belfast. He has been a teacher in Preston, Stoke-on-Trent, Ballymena and Belfast. His poems have appeared in various Irish publications and been broadcast on Radio Ulster, and he has been awarded bursaries from the Northern Ireland Arts Council. *The McGildowney Marine Band* was published by Lapwing Press in 1992.

We would like to thank Dr Mary Hughes, Ulster Scots Language Centre, University of Ulster; Dr Kay Muhr, Northern Ireland Place-Name Project, Department of Celtic, Queen's University, Belfast and Father Finbarr Clancy, SJ, for their advice and expertise.

CONTENTS

The Towers Picture-House

Dorothy Lamour and Greta Garbo and the local manageress Dot
O'Reilly lived in that place
And you had to get in there.
It was class!

Sometimes I had a pass from my father
Since he displayed their posters in his shop:
A lovely piece of white paper that said
'Admit the Bearer'.

'Admit the Bearer': that was me!
Though it was to the Back Stalls once a week
And to the Front Stalls the other time
It was like a passport to another world.

My Uncle Joe was the projectionist and
Once or twice he was at the door
Letting people in and I was very proud of him,
Standing there like James Stewart with Bogart's cigarette.

The most wonderful place in the Towers was the kiosk
Where they sold sweets because it had glass all round
And by the time you climbed the giant steps outside and
Approached you would think you were in Hollywood itself.

Who cares if the Cadbury's Crunch ruined your teeth and
The ice-cream spoiled your cholesterol count;
The magic was there and we were caught up in it
Like addicts: *A'm maybe goin' a break out o' here, like.*

And years later my mother said *why don't you go up*
And take Joe in some ice-cream into the Waveney Hospital
Where he was lying and dying of lung-cancer from the smoking
And I couldn't. I couldn't like I couldn't go to see Madge.

I couldn't break the link that I had with my past and their heyday.
I couldn't watch them die like I watched Jimmy Cagney.
My heart was breaking for the love that they gave me
And the illusion of love and the romance of the Fifties.

Pike-Man

This tackle box is full of lures,
Traces of dead weeds,
Urges of seasons,
Threads of myself alone.

The silver spoon, the copper Mepps,
The double-jointed plug, the Swedish hooks –
Such like I bought myself, and my students
Taught me how to catch a tench on bread.

Terry Eustace fashioned me a soft-action
Pike-rod and I read Barry Rickard's books
And Fred Buller's masterpiece for advice on how
To hunt the big pike.

Yet I grow sad to think that no one
In my family handed down
Any fishing gear to me: they had
No wealth nor the luxury of fishing time.

I sometimes wish that my father had given me
An old cane rod or ancient reel that I could
Talk about with pride; it seems so lonely
Building up a way of life from scratch.

And then I think I'm so selfish with my
Learning: my father never went to school.
He was an orphan from the Lower Falls, cast
At eight years among the sweet people of Harryville.

How can I wish to while away my hours
At one with any other nature,
When he was left alone
To burn the route for rushing through the blood.

In idly doing something true,
Feeling that loneliness,
Stunned at the lording pike,
I become myself.

The Persuader

My father-in-law is full of experience,
Able to feel under the flues of a solid-fuel boiler
Without embarrassment.

He is full of faith, getting on with the job in hand
Even in the face of long neglect – the corrosion of Summer
After a damp Spring clogging the whole caboodle up.

He gets stuck in with the flue-scraper, while I admire
The pale October sun. But he coaxes me along,
Having been through it all before.

I bend an old poker – one leg of a tong, he reminds me,
That belonged to John-Across-The-Water, God rest his soul –
A persuader.

It'll take you sixty years to learn how to change a nappy, says he,
And me pensive about that bloody pike that broke my line under
The boat at Graignamanagh.

Once they had to call the Fire Brigade – his nephew John –
To extricate his elbow from a very tight spot,
Though his wife was quite pleased that it was
Her chimney and not the big breast across the road.

Job, Chapter 22

I found a little snail on the tip of my shoe
When I'd come to sit down from the garden.
And I thought, *Little snail, all the world, NASA and WHO*
Couldn't produce a little beauty like you.

Curl up for your papa, curl up on my shoe:
Stretch along the stitches of my DMs.
For God's sake speak to me: say what a nice bloke
I am to let you go and not crush your brains out
Against the sole of my shoe.

I found a little snail, a baby one, on the tip of my shoe,
And really I don't know what to do
What with smoking and drink and trying to write a great play
And giving my young brother back his old college missal
Because his little baby daughter is ill.

I was reading Job 22, opened randomly for you
My dead mother: Sacred Heart of Jesus have mercy on her soul.

Thou sayest: How does God know? Can he judge through the dark cloud?

Little snail may The Lord bless and keep you,
May he show his face to thee and give thee peace –

Is God not in the height of Heaven? And behold the height of the stars,
How high they are!

I found a little snail on the tip of my shoe and she's still there;
For all the world at home in my study.
'I hope all goes well with you and the test ahead is a success
And Liam is growing bonnier' is what she wrote on the card.
May the Lord bless you little snail – where have you gone?

I see you slithering on the floor, reluctant; somebody will step on you.
I cannot cope with you. Except to put you back in the grass.
It's late. Everybody is in bed. I'll try little snail.
Goodbye. Here goes. Slide onto the top of this biro.
Come on. There you go. Into the garden shrubs.
I'll go to bed soon. Have another cigarette.

I found you little snail on the tip of my shoe.
And now I've lost you. And I'm growing maudlin.
What else can I do?
My faith failing me; me thinking
Ah, it was only a slug, anyway.

Craigbilly

Over the grave of this elm log
Long ago cut down
Rises into the lake of my native land
A fresh green shoot carrying its head
Like a holy sacrament for this blind world.

On Cemetery Sunday once, we walked between the graves
Singing hymns, spreading sweet-smelling incense.
The peaceful Braidside soothed the dead
As they smiled from under their grey mounds.
Tiny churches, basalt stone walls,
Immured our spirits, warmed our hearts
Like hayricks of sun stacked in the water's depth.

New life is fearful, all of us newcomers in our own land.

Bernadette (died 1942, aged 1$\frac{1}{2}$ years)
for David Herbison

The hills are sae bonnie
In the infant spring,
Her firstlings under slaethorn an' hazel.

By Craigbilly Hill, by me mother's side,
She lies so still.

Ah! the Braid Hills are sae bonnie!

Up Caugherty
I trudged – in truth
Afraid to see my sisters' grave.

Oh, I stood for a brave while,
A mountain thrush my company.

Ah! the Braid Hills are sae bonnie!

Lay me where my parents lie
I heard my brother sigh,
'Til in my dreams I see them smile

By Caugherty, by heaven's side,
To bide so still.

Ah! the Braid Hills are sae bonnie!

By Craigbilly Hill, by my father's side,
We shall all lie soon; and the Braid Hills still bonnie.

Neighbour

We're a thrawn people
But kind:
Gae us a chance
To show you what we're like.
I'll tell you
Half in your language
An' half in mine.

At me fether's funeral
I met a brave person;
A Paisleyite to you,
An old neighbour of mine.
His beliefs forbade him
Entering a Catholic church:
He couldnae take part
In any Catholic Service.
He stood on the roadside
Outside Craigbilly Chapel,
His umbrella assisting him
In what to do with his hands.
He loved my mother;
He respected my father.
Maybe he liked us,
Maybe he didnae.
He braved himself,
His beliefs and elders;
He overcame all awkwardness
To shake my hand
And walk with me
In my grief.

Dinnae worry. He has passed away
To meet his good wife;
To meet The Lord Jesus.

Wilbur and I had lived
Side by side for a while
In a housing estate in our home town.
Old Sandy, his father,
Had talked to me as a son.

Yer slow but yer sure,
So dinnae fret about the clippers,
Tak them al' day.

Dinnae tak tae me aboot
Religion:
Dinnae lecture me al' day
Aboot Charity!

From Ballycastle
for Jacko, Rest in Peace

The plan was to borrow the brother's boat
And blast our way over to Toraigh
So that Jacko or Carlo could do his
Geography project 'somewhere different'.

But it was only a romantic notion,
As in *Let me have an island, Lord,*
When autumn comes, and row me over
To Toraigh, to the end of Ireland or

The beginning of your own kingdom.

Wolf Catches the Rathlin Ferry

Yon gypsy girl stooped through an open window
In my bottle-green conservatory
And I imagined from her eyes
She asked could I find in bitter weeds
And unsalted rough meat enough strength
To lie down with her: *oh surely be,* say I.
Can you take me in the damp and cold hedge,
She asked, *without wailing like an injured fox?*
Oh no trouble, says I.
Can you walk twenty miles through mist and rain
And sleep in the draught of a snowstorm?
I can, says I.
She was after gold and I gave it,
Thinking I might become a gypsy and surely have her.
Can you leave Carey for good, she begs,
Say goodbye to your oul' trodden paths?
I cannot, says I.
Then you'll never make the gypsy and away with her
Round by Carraig Dhubh leaving me alone
To face the cruel swirls of Slough-na-Morra.

On the boat I drank to her brown skin,
The swell of her bosom, her dark eyes.
What is more beautiful, I thought me,
Than the slope of a blackbird's breast
And her picking up crumbs for her young?
Ah, you can swim in the same river, but
You cannae step into the same sheugh twice.

Ulster Gothic

The Rossmore Estate is now a Country Park
Set in a Gothic landscape. Or so my
Buddhist friend assures me. She has had a good look at
The basket-of-eggs topography of the drumlins, the trees
Twisted back on themselves along hedgerows, their gnarled
Bodies pledging eternal witness to suffering and torture.

There is something badly wrong here.

I know the drumlins. I have lived amongst them in Lecale.
Farm houses hug the dry tops and small lakes mark the badly
Drained hollows. Roads do their best to follow esker ridges
But these are few and far between. The coarse fisherman
Finds tench in the muddy bottoms of the drumlin lakes, their
Orange eyes caught at dawn on bread or worm or maggot.
The green fear of the carboniferous, the pike, rages and
Glides round sudden depths and solitary perch seek deep holes.
Bream and roach and rudd abound in what is a paradise of sorts.

Above sea level, above lake level, above and below this gothic sky
There is another story, to be sure. This is not Lecale.
This is no Downpatrick.
There is something badly wrong here, in Monaghan.

I have felt it before and wished myself in Cavan.
I have fished Lough Bawn and hired a cottage from the Tennisons.
I have felt this is an odd landscape. Odd. Something has happened
Here that the trees and birds and slopes and soil will not let us forget.

What is it? Too many estates, perhaps. But then in Down there are
Estates. The whole country is in estates. Jesus. We know all this.
The estates in Down are alive though, either as parks or ongoing farms
Or whatever it is about them that makes them seem almost bearable.
And there are estates I know in Antrim which fed the people in hard times.
And there are estates which have decayed into bird droppings with my blessing.

And this estate here with its lake and paths and trees and gardens is not
Too big and has been left to the nation as a writers' centre. Good must
Come of such a gift, to be sure.

Yet there is something badly wrong here.

I don't mean the misty weather; the clouds coming down as if they were
Hedges. No. Nor the lack of sun or light or relief from these small hollows.
Jesus. I'm not comparing this place to Antrim. I'm not saying it could do
With a mountain or two. Or a cliff or a whiff of the sea.
I'm not saying the people are odd. One drunk accosted me in Cootehill
And called me over, *God*, he said, *I was sure it was Noel Purcell himself.*
But his cloud is not that of the northern sky: it has no sky to hang in.

This is a gothic place, says Brigid that lives, like Hannah, on the high Pennines and has
Climbed the Himalayan ridges. *The snow*, she says, *lies deep over my house
That I can't get out for three months at a time.* But she can see the sky
Through her front window and has no need to cry for mountains.

There is something badly wrong here.

Perhaps the people had nowhere to escape: no mountain hideouts
To turn to, to run to in times of need.
The trees that have twisted themselves into shapes
Belonging more to Transylvania than home. Where would you hide
Here, my friend, that know the handbooks of guerilla war?
Deep in the perch retreat? In your dreams where evil can easily
Penetrate? In the church up the road? Among the yews arranged
So neatly in the burial-ground of the Rossmores? No. You'd twist
Back inside your self, my friend, like these trees.
And me.

Our Own Ghosts

We were trying to get over the border
Before nightfall,
Into the freedom of Leitrim.

The boys felt like Hallowe'en revellers
Chasing the sun up Vesuvius,
Losing themselves in their own country.

A red light hung suddenly in mid-air
And put the heart across us: only
A frontier farmer herding his cows.

It hits the neck muscles, this anxiety
Of wishing for streams, lakes to fish in,
In peace.

This is a space station!
Petrol and pubs pock-mark the landscape.
You need a full tank and the boot down.

Next morning, white lanes in the mirror,
Shaving in the reflection of water
Cold enough to be its own ghost.

We search for the hide of the perch –
A deep pocket, free of the day,
Rich in the easiness of lake-gas.

Corraín Tuathail

I lay on top of Corraín Tuathail
In perfect summer bliss
'Til a big honey bee, hovering
Three feet above,
Coaxed me, one eye still closed,
One elbow raised along the bronze,
To ask little questions of the mountain:
How high can this be? Is she closer
To heaven than me?

I didn't know
Bees could fly lighter than spirits,
Above the heads of mountains.

I got up and looked across The Reeks,
Their knives drawn, their feet deep in tarns
And white streams. I could see Killarney,
Two girls nursing a Beetle and our picnic,
But no clouds nor trees nor mist nor pale shrouds.

I supposed it was always thus, here;
No bombs, no needless suffering, no nothing.
Heaven below and heavens above
On the first day of the summer holidays.

First Love

Bobby Shafto's gone to sea,
Silver buckles on his knee,
He'll come back and marry me,
Bonnie Bobby Shafto.

I cover my Canon Starwriter with a green cloth
Carefully folded, so that the children won't disturb
My machine. Below the cloth is an old velvet curtain,
Folded in turn over a wad of writing-paper
Left like a pall over ciborium.
So priest-like the whole procedure, it makes me think
Of infants practising for their First Communion.

We were all kneeling at the altar rails
With Miss McLaughlin pretending to be the priest.
She touched each proffered tongue with the handle
Of a pair of scissors; tapped each tongue
As a dry run. All I could see were her legs under her
Tweed skirt and I could feel a great sense of security.
Our hands were joined under imaginary altar cloths,

And I knew that Bobby Shafto never would return.

Talking with My Brother

Are these souls, he asked me, strangely,
As we walked along the Devenagh Burn
– I could see tiny heathers twitching in the wind –
Souls of our fore-folk,
Their love luring us on?

He had that odd way of asking questions
– I thought the stream was shining –
Not really expecting an answer and often
About death and dying and the afterlife
Or his wife or favourite daughter.

Are these waves? he asked, and in truth
I was feeling wanzing weak. I could see
The family face amongst the rippling lilies,
Our tumbling selves against the throng.

There he was, preaching from the pulpit
In that tiny chapel – Father Scullin lying
Outside the door, lonely I thought,
Forgotten under a drab grey stone,
Breezes from Glenarm Bay his company.

By Curlswater he fished for pike and
I used to wonder why he never asked me
Would I like to try a cast or two or
Had I a brain at all or any kind of knack.

And so it would go on for years that I
Would follow him to watch the bikes or
Cheer at The Clock for Ballymena United
Or feed his banties, go for corn.

I can hear him yelling up our street:
I've got a brother! A wee brother!
Oh 1943 was sweet! He simply jumped for joy
And I just listened as he told me how
– apart from the Rollers –
He loved me almost as much as his homing pigeons.

Barbara Flowers

Strange how women grow
Very like other women
Until there's not much
Difference between them
Except their eyes

Though it was more
The beauty of their names
Made me think how women
Become like seals
To throw the water and the light
Off their naked bodies,
Californian sea-lions
Most beautiful in Belfast Zoo.

Take Mary 'Maude' Maginty for instance,
What a gorgeous name;
Or Kitty O'Rourke;
Or Sally Field – field as in meadow,
She used to say –
Or Barbara Flowers.

Now, Barbara Flowers
Could charm the swans
Off of a lake or,
In a different mood,
Those same eyes could draw
The ducks off the Waterworks.

Irish Hare

Just around the time
You might be hoping for a sign,
Unconsciously,
The hare appeared
Very far down in my garden.

Like an omen of goodwill;
Of the hereafter;
That life had a meaning
Beyond;
The hare came up to my window,
And I was startled too.

Death had struck.
She lay like an old doll
On a sofa.
The family gathered around
And I could sense their fear:
Here he comes!

Wasn't I the soft one,
In tears.
And isn't it in my garden
The hare appears.

Canon Law

I was sitting three rows from the Front
At the end of a pew in the chapel
When Kitty O'Rourke did a bit of a bow
And a half-genuflection with her hand on the post
Of the seat: she hit me a dunt with the tail of her coat
And murmured something about there being plenty of room
And I prayed in the roast of smells that odours of
Incense and flowers from the altar made with fox furs
And travelling whiffs of midden-yard fleas.

But her kindly oul' face was quickly forgotten for there
Was more entertainment at hand: the late Phely Keenan
Arrived at Mid-Aisle and did a wee slider like her:
He'll be late for his own funeral the congregation were thinking
And just as the Canon had started the Mass: *Introibo ad altare Dei* …
Up came a loud roar from the Back and all but the fox-furs
Had craned their necks round to get a good look at the dornach
That had let out the shout *Up Donegal*, and nearly everybody
Smiled but the Canon was sore that up the Far Aisle
Bold Drunk Alec himself had stolen his thunder.

Yet soon enough the Church asserted her authority for the Canon
Had reached the pulpit by some devious route: I often had
Wondered what kept him so long between the altar and the metal
Steps up: maybe his holiness, or his legs weren't so good.
But when he got up he was mildly theatrical, all moaning and grunt;
Very mysterious in his vestments to us youngsters up Front;
But to the Back, they couldn't care less, with their cards and
Their cant against every last word that he mumbled.

J. B. McAllister, Esq., 10 guineas, and he gave the side of his head
A stroke for each guinea in satisfaction that things in the world
Of All Saints, Ballymena, Diocese of Connor, Cill Chon Riaghla,
In the County of Antrim, were as they should be. The Litany
Went on and on in a Gregorian Chant 'til it came to my father:
One Pound – always *One Pound.* And I was proud that his name
Was so far up the Collection: not down among the half-crowns
Or the dreaded two-bobs or the poor one-shillings.

And then we all stood up for the Canon to give us his blessing:
Ite, Missa est.
        Deo gratias.
                Benedicat vos omnipotens Deus, Pater,
Et Filius, et Spiritus Sanctus – and we ran for the side door

To escape to the air, and the grass and the trees: all was well
In the world and life could go on now that the Canon had read his wee list.

The Mid-Antrim 150

My brother took me to my first race
And the trick seemed to be
To find a gap in the hedge along a fast section
And get your legs pushed in.

Our heads were hanging out, almost touching
The Ballygarvey Road and we could see
Many other heads, like spring moles, testing
Sight and distance before the start.

There was a strange pregnant silence

Then the unmistakable roar of Nortons,
The slow men first, then Jones, then Rensen.

After the first lap another silence filled
With the smell of racing oil,
Toffees and adjustments to the hedge;
The mind full of numbers, fairings and speed.

Rudges, B.S.A.s and Velocettes,
Moto Guzzis, Triumphs and Aerials;
McCandless, Templeton and D'Agostino
Shot an old coach road into the realm of magic.

Years became seconds: gods without mortal nerves
These braves. The whine of newfangled machines,
Yamahas and Suzukis, threatened to replace the music
Of Ralph and Malcolm and McCosh our local hero.

My brother took me to my first race,
And still the trick seems to be
To find a gap along a fast section
And get your legs pushed in.

Mair Fadge

They were a' oot
But the wee fella
An' Jeannie an' me
Set fer to get at it

So damn me hadn't I
Slung him up on the ceilin'
Wae a load o' fadge
'Ud feed a pig

An' her keen to get on
Wae it nae houlin'
Back her big chest
Hangin' o'er me

Like some vision o'
The world ye wudnae see
If ye lived to be as oul'
As yer grannie

But sweet Mollie McCree
Didn't the wee bugger
Get peckish an' stick oot
His heed an' scream doon

Mair fadge or oot I coom!
An Jeannie awa' like a hen
That knew it was Christmas
An' me sittin' there

Wae me da's shoes on
An' his best troosers
Poor Jeannie doon the rowad
An' me fit to be tied!

Norman

1

I was walking early
Of a Sunday morning
Round the streets of my old town

Not a soul about
The wind blowing last night's litter
Round the lamp-posts

Looking in the windows
For something of the old days
Hoping to find some clues

As to why I was here
Relaxed
Back in the streets of my childhood

I was looking in Hedley Ferguson's
And Simon McCrory's
And Charlie Caulfield's

It felt good after a spell
In Preston, Belfast and Stoke
To be at home

2

I met an old neighbour
Walking like myself
A chance meeting

I spoke to him softly
About his mother because I'd
Met him years ago

And we had a drink
In a wayside bar and grew sad
About the old days

And I said I was sorry
About his father dying so young
And leaving them all so suddenly

Even though they'd all been
In the B-Specials and I'd
Looked on in a kind of stunned

Wonderment about the guns
And wee Jack shouting
Go out an' get them, boys!

I found it a strange coincidence
That the two of us should be
Wandering around the empty town

Looking for ourselves in the windows.

Parish Gravedigger

Our friend Sammy is usually busy
But hardby, half to himself,
His true eye more for his dog

— There's no much o' thon yin left, John —
Revving up a Norton,
Sending a skirt flying.

Wasn't he the quare boyo in his day,
Flapping wings and roaring hedges
To Caugherty moss-side romances.

There's plenty o' room in there,
For they dinnae last long.
But his eye has turned misty.

Not the whiskey nor the drouth:
More being-beads of time,
A field of family names.

Suddenly he laughs from deep,
Coughs and splutters dates,
Talks history.

Poor oul' Master Loy lies here.
There's Father Green himself,
Girls fleeing from his thorn.

Kitty O'Rourke has shit her shirt
And hung it out to dry.
He doubles over in stitches,

Knowing I'd rather laugh than cry —
Knowing I know the rest —
Knowing why I came.

Rum, Jim Lad!

A thousand barrels of dark rum!

Late last century a ship sank somewhere
In the Irish Sea
And deep in her hold
Lay a full cargo of McKibbin's Rum (Est. 1871).

A thousand barrels of dark 'Jamaicy' rum!

By now it's probably full of plutonium
From Sellafield.

So even if we hire the *Evelyn Maude*
And put together a bit of an expeditionary crew
Out of Kintyre
To explore yon seabed down to a hundred fathoms;
And even if we skirt the overfalls of Slough-na-Morra
And avoid Atlantis steering by the Northern Star,

We could all end up dead.

But, a THOUSAND barrels!

My Littlest

for Brian and Ruth

In a dream last night I heard her cry
For her grandfather
And I could only think of my own father
Crying out in his orphaned sleep: *mammy!*

She had lost the head of her mermaid,
Lost her friend Michael, met a witch,
Climbed to the top of the tree ladder,
Hurt her finger, wrist, knee, and side
Of her poor head; had a cot fall on her;
Gone through her brother hating her,
Her Barbie lost, her spaghetti brown.

Could you get a cat and a rabbit and
A gerbil soon please. And her teacher
Had hit her. Mrs Walker is always
Hitting her but she likes Mrs Brown very well
Because she shows her belly button.

And could she have something to eat and
A drink of water and some raw pasta shells
And a necklace and a lolly and a glass of milk.

What are you coughing about in there, she says,
All three years of her, to her grandfather.

In a dream last night I heard their conversation –

Him sitting in there in his shed, stoking up his pipe,
And telling her stories and wishing that
We could know how much the dead love the living.

42

Radio Cachker

She hit him a clash on the ear with the side of her hand
And you could hear the crack of it all over Larne.

He'd taken four big cachkers at a time and laid them up,
One in his right hand and three lined up his left arm

And paced up the back garden and let fly at the chicken house
He'd built for his brother and her standing there

Watching him do it and me on my holidays from Ballymena
For the fortnight, aged eight.

She threw her leg through the wire of the garden fence
And socked him squarely on the jaw

And then followed with a beautiful right and I thought
She was a tough cookie and still do.

She had been brought up rough and ready like,
The middle of a big Catholic family

And bred in bloody poverty down below
Caugherty, outside Ballymena.

She was my aunt Katie and I loved her
Like a boy might love his aunt

That had water barrels outside her Carnlough cottage
On the Whitehill Road and strange sea captains calling

And them all talking about the weather and sounding
Of Scotland and fishing round the Black Rock

And Old Robert spitting and cursing and swearing
That he'd never make it.

Whatever he was making I didn't know and anyway
Up the road was a tropical forest with strange big plants

Covered in white dust and beyond was trout country
And Cranny Lake that I could never imagine finding.

And there was strange food: all wollicks and
Boiled sea creatures that these people relished.

But suddenly they lived in Larne and things were never the same:
It was all sausages and tripe and fighting

Though there was the flying of the imitation model aeroplanes
Over the side of Drumalis cliff

But my cousin Robert insisted I was from tuffy-toon
And I resented this and fighting was the order of the day.

And then just as suddenly as in a vapour as the Bible says
My aunt was sitting there with my mother and me

On Fry's Road in Ballymena in the Seventies
And we were having a few jars

And they talked the night through about the old days
And the Black and Tans lifting their bedclothes

And the terrible hunger for life that hit them as girls
Growing up in the Twenties and Thirties

And about how happy they'd been escaping to dances
And how Father Green had had a blackthorn stick

To beat them along the roadsides home away from evil influences
And about how many Golden Wonders they could eat.

And then my aunt fell ill and life for those poor souls
Was continuing to be as hard as only life can be

And I went to see Katie being buried in Larne and talked
To the functionary priest at his door about Garron Tower

And such things but what the hell could you say
When you realised the state her family were in:

Half exported to petty poverty in England
And half crippled in body or mind here at home.

And Jesus you could grow sad yourself about the old days
When they were alive and fighting, so to speak.

Stella Maris

STAR OF THE SEA
PRAY FOR THE SINNER
PRAY FOR ME

I can see everything that's happening,
He said,
Clear as a bell
All the way from Whitehead
To Lissan.

It was part of a conversation
I had recently
In the Greenvale Hotel, Cookstown,
After the funeral of Margaret Donaghy.

Strange that a man should live his life
An alien in his own country.
Having drunk away a farm
He had to banish himself
And go to work for I.C.I.
And I knew another like him
Who got education instead of the land.
Sad how fate awaits us most strongly
When our parents die and what we thought ours
Is not ours at all but merely given.

Like the simple truth that I was taught
On my mother's knee:
Not I Lord, but Thee.

Or like a man with land
No matter how poor or marginal
Will have a headstone:
Joseph Donaghy, Killybaskey.
That fixes him more than any church.

And so the real poor are those like me
That know they've lost their birthright,
Their land or farms.
We are the ones that had only the church
And the church has a lot of land, enough
To bury you and you and you, my friend.

In Ballycastle once I heard a priest –
The one that christened me though
That was in another parish –
Sing in happy chant this hymn
And I was close to tears then
As now:

STAR OF THE SEA
PRAY FOR THE WANDERER
PRAY FOR ME.

A Great Teacher

There is a knack to lighting old candles, their limp wicks:
Turn them upside down and wait for a new neck to form;
Though holy new ones or special ovals with red rim
Will set you back a bob or two in Carey Chapel:
Place your bets in the wall box beside the Virgin's statue.

It was after walking Emer over to see her great-aunt's grave,
Its sandy headstone with the double-humped shoulders
Erected by past pupils of Dolly McCaughan, P.T.,
That I've taken tonight to the candles again in my shed:
Two, then a third to keep the odd number, the Trinity.

I've tried in vain to understand the internal workings
Of a big Queen Anne oil-lamp, a brass affair from the auction;
Failed to reconstruct a green mini made in Taiwan and
Even a double-wick procured in Sharpe & McKinley's
Wouldn't do the trick for the lamp my mother bought me.

At Tornaroan Lower the candle wax melted, stuck to my fingers
Like latex, dripped on to the Hevea Brasiliensis floor;
Reminding me in pain of the magister's pale creamy skin,
His T.T., celibate, frail waxy hands around
Soft parts of my underchin, the steamy neck glands.

The Chapel School

in god there are three persons
god the father god the son and god
the holy ghost so how many gods are
there three god you stupid boy (wallop!)
the prizes came back from cadburys
and all you had to do was scratch
off the face of the Queen from
the little tin box to get the chocolate
we were staring at this clay model
of a monastery and all i could think
of was deirdre delargy's legs

Miss McVeigh sent me over
With Master Molloy's coffee cup
And I noticed the skin on top of the milk
As I ran up the stone steps in the yard.

Miss McLaughlin had taught us well
How to knock the door and say *please sir*
Without Dick's whole class falling into stitches
And Black Bess having to come out.

Con Magee had been stabbed in the side
Of his new plastic jacket in class
And two dead rats had been found
Hanging suspiciously

From the one tree in the school.
We had been terrorised for half an hour
By Alec, one of the big boys. He had a knife
And was fourteen and knew how to use it.

And one of the seniors had got a girl
Up the spout and was getting married soon.
But we were concentrating on the teams
That Jock had picked for touch rugby.

Trojans, Greeks, Spartans and Athenians
Were the names and I was captain of the Trojans
And we won the spellings and the sums as well
As the football in the lower yard.

Dick came over to try to teach us singing
And Davy hung upside down at the window
As lookout and when he shouted
Dick's coming it was bedlam for a while.

Geraldo showed me how to open my mouth
And pretend to be singing the words but
Even then I didn't make the choir though
Geraldo did and lived to regret it.

The place was all full of old desks with ink-wells
And antique nibs that leaked onto the poor paper.
We spent most of the time doing potato presses
Or practising handwriting like ancient scribes.

Jock taught us hygiene, how to cut our nails
Straight and brush our teeth up and down and
Master Parkes explained how difficult the abbot
Might be if you were a novice in a monastery.

One of the parents was objecting
About the smell of the lavatory and
The rats eating the lunches but Molloy
Said something about it being good enough

For young Paddy Murphy though he left
For a public school in England soon afterwards.
I spent so much time cleaning McCracken's
Moped and getting lost doing his groceries

Down Broughshane Street that there wasn't space
To worry about whether or not
The scones in our play about the Broon Family
Were like concrete and dangerous to throw.

I had a stand-up fight which lasted an afternoon
But P. J. McEvoy brought in so many blackjacks
That we bluffed the qualifying sums well enough
To pull the wool over Jock's eyes for a while.

But we were sad when we met that day after Mass
In Jock's house with the successful results;
We were all going to St. MacNissi's in September
Except Danny Docherty who had more cow sense.

We were for the chop and we kind of knew it.
No more Miss McLaughlin or Miss McVeigh,
One big class of fifty of us competing
For light and air and love and attention.

Rectory Ranger

for David McWilliams

He gave everything to the smallest thing;
always himself,
he knew far better than me that earth
is made of heaven.

Where I would like to think of local
names of places wafting over me
like a soothing breeze,
he sang of Peggy Sue, Pearly and sweet
sexy ladies.

We both lived outside the history
of this place;
where I wanted to vanish into some
mythical heart of Ireland,
he said *don't banish yourself
from your own heart.*

He's really made the big time now,
the rest of us hoping to get there
by candlelight.

The Royal Victoria Hospital
for Emer

In the Neutral Zone her knight
Sees only real stars:
Tom Faggus has tethered his mare
Just over there where they bring in the dead.

I'm fine, having a smoke, chatting
Up the blonde in the crude denims.
I tell her I'm writing a poem for my daughter
Lying in intensive care. She says her son
Has cerebral palsy and is in and out every
Other week: she has her own room to sleep over.
Christ what have I got to complain
About that might have fostered my pearl out
Away from this city, somewhere further north
Amongst her own people. I might have.
I might have joined the ribbonmen years ago
And wished well of the local landlord.
I might have taken a gun and shot
A few crows or pigeons except I quite like them.

But the word is she's all right. No brain damage.
She'll see the stars again, in that right eye.

I could murder a pint right now, in the Angler's Arms,
For I don't know if I can stick the neutral zone
Much longer, the night being full
Of green stars from Ireland.

Road into Carna 1964

it was pitch black, warm-dark,
the girls' laughter lilting,
their young arms linked,
the girls close.
the air was balmy, there was
a kiss or two after the black
drink in Paidin Ban's.
the bacon was on, *The Man
From Nova Scotia* the story,
in soft Connemara Irish.

and the morning sweet, the bread
warm; Eileen's mother stooping
over the hot oven, palming the
big loaf onto the table.
Padraic, the clerical student,
was doing his best to pretend
not to know about the girls kissing
in french.

I was talking to the brothers
McKernan who were coming up to free
The North, the livelong day spent
inexpensively on their sofas.
I had a different bike each day
left at the gable of the house
to take me to Muighnis or Kilkieran.

if I could have another go at my life,
their lives,
I would freeze it then: rowing over
to MacDara's island with Eileen;
thinking of her home table full of us
having dinner, chatting away;
playing at the academic researcher
while only finding myself at home.

when I went back the house was empty.
Eileen dead; Eileen's mother dead;
Eileen's two brothers dead;
everything modernised.
Eileen's father dead.
oh sweet Jesus save us all.
I was too young.
I knew nothing.

I was stupid.
Wet behind the ears.
I loved them dearly but
I didn't know how much I loved them.
They loved me but I didn't need them
At the time: I had my father and my mother
And a career ahead.
I hadn't the balls to stay for ever:
If I had stayed we would all have lived for ever.
Hugh O'Flaherty told me, that in a dream
I had come to Muighnis and for whatever reason
Saved my soul by living among them
For the rest of my mortal days.

Madge

Each love gave her a new life,
A new virginity. But to some
Her death improved her.
Why did she give herself so much,
So much each time?

Augh. What could ail it.
As like as not we'd have fought
To the bitter end. Heartsick,
I couldn't bear to see her die.
Some earlier sin was mine.

As you've probably heard, I'm banjaxed,
Living in the back of beyond;
On the blatter every day, on the binge too often.
Catch yersel' on my friends will say,
But man dear, I was dying about her.

Johnny-3-Tongues

Boys-a-dear but you're the coorse christian,
   quo' she,
An' me, only a cub, admiring the cut of her.
Ach, I'd said something daft
About her catching her death of cold
In *that* fur.

It was dayligone an' I was to keep dick
   for a shillin',
So willin' to act the little prick
When a right dornach, an eedyit of a fellow but hearty,
Came moochin' about as if he was somebody.

I lets a gulder out of me:
Ye gobshite, I'm her da!
For fright he hunkers doon like a jinny wran
Not knowing whether to sit or run.
Ah, I says, more to mysel',
An tú fein atá ann?

Heyday

In a kind of waking dream –
Beyond our attic window
And on top of McNally's roof
Where I used to spit and drive
Five racing cars –
There he was, my brother that was the human race to me,
Chatting away, doing an obvious camera shoot,
Oblivious to my cries
Of *Patsy! Patsy!*

It was a kind of waking dream
For I was sleeping in my sickroom
Worrying about dying soon,
Leaving my little children.

He scraped his chair on the blue veins
Of the roof, like Gregory Peck turning sun
And camera to his better cheek,
To his girlfriend on Carnlough Beach.
Strong in sinew, virile, he was happy:
He had no need of me.

And then I thought, I'm allowed
To see him, but not he me –
He's gone, he's dead, but in immortal life;
And someone has sent his picture to me from that place,
To McNally's roof, my childhood den.

I turned my head where I lay to ease
My pain, supposing the dream a far-back day,
The hour itself a ghost …

So soon, it seemed, dawn came,
But down our chiselled names
March's chilly raindrops plough.

Alma Mater

The alarm clock at cock-shout
Clattering its brains out
Awoke me to the morning's
Gentle presence through the room.

I was practising mental prayer,
Saying the Gloria very slowly,
But in the silent pauses my
Mind was wandering upwards

As very quietly I walked
In the sunshine with my friend
Dermot along the lone-rock
Limestone road behind the sea.

The wee field was bathed in sunshine
And light passing like a lance
Across Dunmaul failed to stir the boys
Still sleeping in the old dorms below.

It was beyond an hour 'til breakfast
When we reached the Dog's Grave
And the Coachman's Path led us easily
Downwards and astray for a while …

And then I caught the rhythm
Of the prayer as Fitzy taught me
And it allowed the longer spaces
Between the words

In … no … m … in … e
D … o … m … in … e

Ballymena United

bond

trevorrow   *johnstone*

brown   *lowry*   *cubbit*

egan   *forsyth*   *mcghee*   *mccrae*   *russell*

In the early Fifties there we were
At war each evening with the boys from Guy's School:
Fairhill's stony ground yielding free ammunition
And its many exits and entrances escape routes
In what were quick skirmishes; for both sides,
According to Geraldo our Chapel giant,
Had to prepare ambushes for the Academy Prep,
A right bunch of little softies.

In the People's Park we played football under Spenser's statue:
Street teams doing battle in disused hard courts,
Knees and nets full of holes; pullovers for goalposts;
The crowd roaring as Hill Street led Springwell 52-48.
An old hairy tennis ball like the one Peter Docherty
Did the messages with allowed us to copy our heroes
Right down to the shirt over the trousers like Charlie McMullan
In the second half for Ballymena United.

Across the Park in the proper courts the children of the Prep
Played Wimbledon and sometimes we gazed in through the netting
In complete wonderment at the posh gear and confident cries
Of Wallace McMaster & Co., their apparent oblivion
As they dragged themselves off court and their coloured towels
Dripping to the specially built pavillion
Like so many swans on the Park Dam.

Though he wasn't an Eric Trevorrow or a Jimmy McGhee
We were lucky that Stanley Parke, the keeper's son,
Played for us as we found a Wembley
Between the holly bush and the beech tree,
And when the park bell went
We were oblivious too!

Greenlough

I had taken a notion of visiting Tony and Vedar
In Portglenone
And by way of killing two birds with
One stone
Dropping in on long lost country cousins.

In those days, long ago, the classmates
Were novices;
Tony making great pocs with an imaginary
Hurl,
Insisting on the existence of Heaven.

Since Vedar wasn't allowed visitors,
Not yet,
Uncle John and I rowed along the dark river
For pike,
Admiring two damson trees by Clement's Hill.

My aunt's cheeks were like old roses
In bloom;
You could tell she was happy among fields,
Hens and ducks,
Despite the drudgery, the gurning granny.

Tony's the Abbot these days, Vedar a hermit
Near Garron Tower;
And I help to carry my aunt's coffin
Past plum trees,
A power of grandchildren round Greenlough.

Parish Sports Day

Coming round the big sweep of the final last bend
I could spot the two girls hanging over the wire:
They knew I'd won the 100 yards and
They'd watched me fly through the 200 too –
I'll tell you it was well before we found
That cache of cigarettes in the Dispensary –
But the flags were out at Hugomount
For the Parish Sports and the man in charge
Was Master McCracken, a likely lad
Who set the junior handicaps and let out the yell
That started us off

Though he had to smile too at the toffs
Like J.B. McAllister for there was a big
Crowd of local nobs talking to the Canon
Or even priests and local schoolteachers
Like Miss McVeigh, Jock Scally and Dick Molloy.

There were stalls of buns and cakes and cream
And the most amazing sight I've ever seen:
Paddy Murphy himself giving out the dough
In handfuls to schoolchildren dancing around
'Til all the coppers and shillings and pence
Were spent quickly on Caulfield's ice-cream cones
Or sliders.

But in the 440 I was severely curtailed for
McCracken had put me at scratch to the field
And on the first lap I had only caught up
With some tiddlers and had to run wide as a gap
To get through for they knew there was silver
At stake and everyone of them wanted that
Five bob for the winner or a shilling the place.

It was when the girls shouted I felt the oul surge
That went through me like ice that was warm and aglow
And I'll never forget their wee faces that showed
Love or maybe their worship you know:
COME ON MADUKIAN THE ONE-AND-ONLY!